ADVERTISING
ALVIS
1920-1966

Compiled by
DANIEL YOUNG

1991
Published and distributed by
P4 Spares
60 Woodville Road
London NW11 9TN
(081-455 6992)

ISBN 1 873078 05 6

Preface

Very few British marques have the same claim to genuine prestige and imposing style as Alvis. In particular, the pre-war sports saloons and open tourers have an almost unparalleled charm and character which makes Alvis cars incredibly desirable today.

For this reason I have chosen Alvis for this latest album, as a sequel to my collections on MG, Riley and Rover. As in the past, I have prefaced the material with an illustrated history of the marque.

Once again, my sincerest thanks are due to Brooklands Books who have, as always, assisted me most generously in the preparation of this volume which was, in no small way, inspired by their own *Gold Portfolio*. It is my sincere hope that this modest offering will complement their excellent publication.

D.Y.

Also in this series:
Advertising Rover 1904-1964 (104pp)
Advertising MG 1929-1955 (96pp)
Advertising Riley 1906-1968 (96pp)

Front cover:
Advertising the handsome new TA21 3-litre Saloon, 1950

THE TALE OF THE INVERTED TRIANGLE

The story of Alvis cars is virtually the life-story of Thomas George John, the 'Welsh wizard'
who began manufacture in 1920 of one of the most beautiful and best loved British marques

Right: a front-wheel drive Alvis, the yellow 1½-litre known as 'Tadpole', at Brooklands in 1925. Major C. M. Harvey, the chief works driver, suffered at first from front tyres which came loose, but when this trouble was cured he was able to lap at a speed of 104.41 mph. *Below*: a magnificent example of the 'duck's back' 12/50 of 1926

OF THE MANY new makes of British motor car appearing shortly after World War I, most were 'assembly jobs' using proprietary engines and other bought components. Two major exceptions were Alvis and Bentley, for both fitted engines of their own design and manufacture and, in the long distance international races of the 1920–30 period, Alvis came nearer than any other British make in the 1½ litre class to emulating Bentley achievements in the big car category.

The two marques even had a tenuous common background in the small French DFP car, for the designer of the first Alvis, G. P. H. de Freville, had been manager before the war of Bentley & Bentley in Hanover St, London. That is where W. O. Bentley and his brother H. M., both then in their mid-twenties, had just entered the motor trade and successfully sold DFPs on the strength of W. O.'s competition successes with these cars. The 12–15 hp DFP was a sporting, lively, well-made car, characteristics that both W. O. Bentley and de Freville bore in mind when designing, respectively, the 3-litre Bentley and 10/30 hp Alvis cars.

The presiding genius of Alvis was a Welshman called Thomas George John, who had founded the Coventry firm of T. G. John Limited in March 1919, at the age of 39. When only 31, as a practising marine engineer, he had managed Armstrong-Whitworth's Barrow-in-Furness Shipbuilding Department. During the war he had turned to aviation engineering, being Works Manager of Siddeley-Deasy at Coventry at a time when they were producing Siddeley 'Puma' aircraft engines.

In forming his own company, John took over premises at 17 Hertford St, Coventry, from the Holley Brothers, the American carburettor manufacturers. Initially he continued with carburettor work, moving on to produce 'Electra' single and twin cylinder stationary engines and 50 cc Stafford Mobile Pup scooters, and doing sub-contract work for Indian motorcycles.

The Alvis car was born when John bought the drawings of the 10/30 hp from de Freville together with the name, which de Freville had first used as a trade mark when he was manufacturing light alloy pistons during the war. After he had driven a 10/30 in the 1920 London-Edinburgh Trial (and won a silver medal in what was the make's debut in a major

The first production model of the fwd Alvis appeared in 1928. With all-round independent suspension, it was perhaps the most advanced British car of its time

competition) de Freville himself faded out of the picture so far as Alvis were concerned.

There was nothing unconventional about the rather expensive, high quality, side-valve, 1460 cc 10/30 Alvis. Like nearly all its contemporaries, it did not have front-wheel brakes, although the two-seater versions were fitted with the interesting and very light Morgan 'Zephyr' steel wire-braced all metal bodywork built on lines reminiscent of the construction of the later Italian Zagato coachwork. A contemporary owner described his 10/30 as extremely 'hot' (it would do around 60 mph) and 'above the run of average cars'.

In 1921 T. G. John Limited moved to Holyhead Road, Coventry, and the name of the firm was changed to the Alvis Car & Engineering Company Limited. The factory included offices, two machine shops, assembly and finishing shops and a foundry, although the cylinder heads and blocks had to be bought out at this time. A much lightened 10/30 was entered for the 1921 Coupe des Voiturettes race at Le Mans, driven by the works driver Major C. M. Harvey. Although lying handily behind the three eventually victorious Talbot-Darracqs after only four laps, Harvey then had to retire due to a stone cracking his sump. In the Brooklands 200 Miles Race, two streamlined 10/30 cars averaged only 65.57 mph and 56.17 mph for the race, although Harvey, in the faster car, was said to have lapped at 87 mph in practice.

In 1922 Alvis attempted to enter the bread-and-butter market by manufacturing a reasonably civilised version of the pre-war V-twin air-cooled Buckingham cyclecar, but this did not last very long, output mainly being concentrated on the 10/30 and the bigger bore 1598 cc 11/40 hp, introduced at the 1921 Motor Show, and now reclassified as the 12/40 hp. Production was about a dozen cars a week.

The most significant move in 1922 was the appointment of Captain G. T. Smith-Clarke as Chief Engineer and W. M. Dunn as Chief Designer, John henceforth devoting himself to the business side of the Company. Smith-Clarke's genius can be briefly summed up in the citation which went with the award of the James Clayton engineering prize to him in 1957 (three years before his death), to mark his work in 'the development of mechanisms used in connection with astronomical telescopes and for his services in the field of aero engines and automobile engineering in addition to that

A TE series 12/50 tourer of 1927, with artillery wheels and the upper half of the windscreen divided into two

on mechanical breathing apparatus'. Smith-Clarke, in addition to his contributions to astronomical and hospital equipment research, was also a pioneer in the early days of radio, and experimented in 1923 with radio communication between racing cars and the pit.

'We cannot but consider it one of the classic designs of the time, and it remains of all Vintage sports cars the one which needs least apology'. So wrote Clutton and Stanford of the 12/50 Alvis in their book *The Vintage Motor Car*. The 12/50, which was a development of the earlier Alvis models but fitted with a pushrod overhead valve 1496 cc engine, was the work of Smith-Clarke and Dunn. It put itself on the motoring map with a flourish when a tuned and lightened version, driven by Maurice Harvey, won the classic 200 Miles Race at Brooklands in October 1923, at 93.29 mph. It led home a Brescia Bugatti by over three minutes, the Bugatti being followed by an AC and an Aston Martin, both of which had special racing overhead camshaft engines.

Alvis, like Bentley, was under-capitalised and, despite the 200 Miles Race win and the success of the 12/50 range, a Receiver had to be appointed in July 1924, largely due to a sum of £5000 owing to the coachbuilders, Cross & Ellis.

Fortunately an arrangement was made whereby the creditors agreed that the firm should carry on, and 331 cars were sold in the six months to February 1925, when the Receiver was in possession. Great assistance in these troubled times was rendered by Henlys, the London agents, who were sometimes aghast at John's stubborness in buying expensive machinery to make bits and pieces at Holyhead Road instead of buying them outside.

Front-wheel brakes were an optional extra on the production cars in 1924, when three special 12/50 racing cars were built with Brooklands racing in mind. They had very low, light chassis, gearboxes integral with the engine (unlike the production cars), minimal brakes and differential-less back axles. Maurice Harvey and Frank Halford, later the very famous and distinguished de Havilland aero engine designer, drove the 2-seater versions of these cars (there was also a single-seater) in the 200 Miles Race, but they did not seem to produce their designed performance, finishing 6th and 8th, with the 1923 winning Alvis in 7th place.

However, the new cars had successes in smaller Brooklands races, in sprints and long distance record-breaking. One of them finished up in Australia, earning its owner, Phil Garlick, great fame on the speedways there until he was killed in it at Maroubra Speedway in January 1927.

Most advanced car of the decade

In March 1925, Alvis produced a car which, from the design point of view, proved that the company was considerably more progressive than any other British manufacturer of the decade. In order to evolve an ultra-lightweight, low slung sprint car, they turned to front-wheel-drive, and the fwd Alvis made its competition appearance at Kop Hill Climb two months before Harry Miller produced the first of his famous front-drive racers at the Indianapolis Speedway in the USA.

The new Alvis had a 12/50 engine turned back to front, and the drive was through pot-joints to a reversed de Dion type front axle as on the Miller. The chassis was of duralumin. Sheet duralumin boxed in the bottom of the driving seat, the cockpit and part of the rear of the engine, monocoque style. The rear axle was a straight tube supported by reversed quarter elliptic springs. The car was very low, 3 feet high from

the top of the bonnet and the scuttle to the ground, and very light, only 9.5-cwt, with an engine giving 70 bhp unsupercharged and, it is said, as much as 100 bhp when supercharged. Disc wheels were fitted.

At Shelsley Walsh in May 1925, this car, in un-supercharged form, put up second fastest time of the day with 54.2 seconds to the 53.8 seconds of H. O. D. Seagrave's 2 litre supercharged Grand Prix Sunbeam, and equalled the time of E. Mayner's supercharged 2 litre Grand Prix Mercedes. Running supercharged, the Alvis lapped Brooklands in Harvey's hands at 104.41 mph and set up standing-start British kilometre and mile records for the 1.5 litre class.

Two cars of this type were adapted for long distance racing and were entered in the 200 Miles Race, the drivers being Harvey and the Earl of Cottenham. Though fast, particularly on corners, they were not as fast as the twin-cam Darracqs, which soon overcame the initial lead of the Alvises. Brakes proved to be the Alvis Achilles heel, for Cottenham retired when the heat from his inboard front brakes dried up his differential and seized-up the transmission, whilst Harvey broke a pushrod due to over-revving after using his engine as a brake, and was flagged off at the end of the race.

In 1926 Alvis produced a front-wheel-drive Grand Prix design to the current 1.5 litre formula. The engine was a supercharged straight eight with horizontal valves; the cylinder block, top half of the crankcase and head formed a monobloc casting, which was produced at the Alvis works and was a notable example of the foundryman's art. Suspension was similar to that on the previous fwd cars, but the body and chassis were steel instead of duralumin. Two examples, which had not been ready for the British Grand Prix, ran in the 1926 200 Miles Race. However, Harvey's car retired

In 1929 the six-cylinder engine was increased in capacity from 1879 to 2148 cc, and the new model Alvis was named the Silver Eagle. The car above, a handsome beetle-backed sports, was originally owned by Maurice Harvey

Right: the Speed 25 was introduced in the autumn of 1936. It was the direct descendant of the Speed 20, by way of the 3.5-litre model that had been introduced the previous year. The 3.5-litre engine was effectively a bored-out Speed 20, but with a new crankshaft and other refinements to make running quieter. The Speed 25 retained these refinements, but also kept the Speed 20's low-built appearance. A variety of special bodies could be ordered from coach-building firms; this 1938 specimen, which still has the original hare mascot is apparently by Bertelli

after a third of the distance due to an accident, having averaged 72 mph to the winning Talbot-Darracq's 75.56 mph, and Cottenham retired when his oil pressure gauge registered zero. The 1927 GP cars had twin overhead camshaft engines and independent front suspension, and the driver sat centrally in the chassis. Unfortunately, the cars did not start in the British GP and both retired in the 200 Miles Race after the usual early promise. Like Vauxhall before them, Alvis never had sufficient financial resources to be able to develop their ambitious Grand Prix projects as fully as they wished.

For 1928 a four cylinder, single overhead camshaft, fwd production car was produced in either super-charged or unsupercharged form. Unlike virtually all their British competitors, Alvis designed and built their own Roots-type superchargers, the work of Willie Dunn. The new cars had independent suspension all round and two unsupercharged examples covered themselves in glory at Le Mans in the 1928 24 Hours Race where they won in their class. Another car, supercharged this time, finished 13 seconds behind the winning Lea-Francis in the 1928 Tourist Trophy race.

The last of front-wheel drive

Ten fwd cars were built with 1.5 litre straight eight, supercharged, twin overhead camshaft engines and all-independent suspension by transverse leaf springs, the engines being based on those of the 1927 GP cars. Apart from long distance record breaking at Brooklands, their best racing performance was in the 1930 Tourist Trophy, when the cars filled the first three places in the 1.5 litre class, and one finished the race just behind the victorious 1750 cc Alfa Romeos of Nuvolari, Campari and Varzi. This was the last works Alvis racing appearance, also the last year the fwd cars were made, these rather harsh sporting models having a limited market.

Below: from 1932, four standard bodies for the Speed 20 were offered by Charles Follett Ltd. These were a four-door saloon by Thrupp and Maberley, and three designs by Vanden Plas: a straight-back saloon, a foursome coupé, and this handsome tourer

Meanwhile the 12/50 had had its record breaking and racing successes, notably third place and team award in the 325-miles Georges Boillot Cup race at Boulogne in 1925, and wins in the Six Hours Race and the Four Hours Sporting Car Race at Brooklands in 1927.

Until 1931 the 12/50, in long-stroke touring and short-stroke sporting form, was the mainstay of Alvis sales, but a six cylinder pushrod model was produced in 1927 using the 12/50 chassis, which had lost its original sub-frame in 1926. Intended as a smoother version of the 12/50, in 1929 the capacity of the 'six' went up from 1879 cc to 2148 cc and it was named the Silver Eagle. This was the forerunner of all the successful Alvis 'sixes' of the 30s, notably the 2.5 and 2.7 litre dual ignition Speed 20, the 3.5 litre Speed 25 and the 4.3 litre, as well as the touring Crested Eagle and the Silver Crest.

The sports models were known for good performance, extreme beauty of line and a reasonable price in comparison with their rivals. The 4.3 was, at one time,

Left: a 1964 Alvis
tourer, with elegant
bodywork by the Swiss
company, Graber.
Below: the TE 21 3-litre
coupé of 1965. Between
1950 and 1967, when
production ceased, the
engine was steadily
uprated, from 90 to
130 bhp

the fastest production saloon on the British market
with a maximum of over 100 mph. Technical advances
were a unique all-synchromesh gearbox and independent front suspension (modelled on that of the eight
cylinder fwd models), both introduced in 1933.

The four cylinder line continued through the
12/60 hp of 1931/2, similar to the 12/50, to the handsome though heavier 1.5 litre Firefly, then the 1842 cc
Firebird, and culminated in the more powerful 12/70
of similar capacity in 1937, largely the work of designer
George Lanchester.

T. G. John died in 1946, having added aero engine
and armoured vehicles to car production at Alvis
Limited (as the firm was renamed in 1936), and in the
years to come first the former and finally the latter took
precedence over the cars. The initial post-war Alvis
car, the beam-axle 14 hp, was modelled on the 12/70 hp
and was produced in larger quantities than any other
Alvis model. In 1950 the 3 litre six-cylinder replaced it,
with coil spring ifs and a new pushrod engine.
Traditional Alvis beauty of line was reintroduced
when the Swiss Graber Company designed bodywork
which was standardised from 1958. The six cylinder
engine was increased in power output from 90 bhp in
1950 to 130 bhp in 1967 when production ceased. At
that time a five-speed ZF gearbox and powered
steering were also available, but by then the Alvis was
beginning to be left behind by its rivals in the performance field.

Two Alvis 'might-have-beens', in the advanced
engineering tradition of the front-wheel-drive, were a
3.5 litre V8 with rubber suspension designed by Alec
Issigonis in the 1952–55 period (which had to be
abandoned due to rising costs), and a remarkable mid-
engined design proceeded with after a merger of Alvis
Limited with Rover in 1965. The latter was eventually
killed off after both firms became part of British Ley-
land in 1967.

After T. G. John's death, J. J. Parkes, the father of
Mike Parkes, the Ferrari engineer and racing driver,
became Managing Director of Alvis Limited. The
famous Alvis inverted triangle badge is still to be seen
today on armoured and cross-country vehicles, in
which field Alvis are one of Europe's leading manufacturers.   PH

The Sporting Light Car DeLuxe

Extracts from "THE AUTO," Nov. 25th, 1920.

"The Alvis 10 h.p. chassis was a nice, clean-looking job, of which the most apparent characteristic is the robust construction of the frame, and especially of the sub-frame carrying the radiator, engine and gear-box. It is a light car, not only in engine capacity, but also in the truest sense, in that weight has been eliminated wherever possible, consistently with strength. It is not a cheap car, and nowhere has low cost been studied at the sacrifice of efficiency. Thus, a four-speed gear-box is provided, and both the bodywork and the equipment are of the highest class. The price is not low, by comparison with that of other cars of about the same engine dimensions, but it must be clear that the Alvis is a very special job, designed by an efficiency-specialist. and built to a very uncommon standard both of material and workmanship."

6 to 60 miles per hour guaranteed.

The fastest and best Light Car made.

Manufacturers:
T. G. John, Ltd
Coventry.

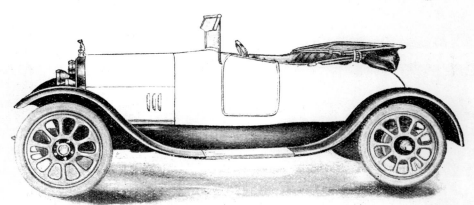

1921 Price : £685
Immediate Delivery
from London & West of England Agents:

R. E. JONES, LTD., 103, New Bond St. W. . . and at Cardiff, Bristol, Swansea & Exeter.

"The Car for the Connoisseur"

ALVIS

Office of
"The Scotsman,"
Edinburgh.
17 May, 1923.

T. G. John, Esq.,
Alvis Car & Eng. Co., Ltd., Coventry.

Dear Sir,

May I take the liberty of writing you a personal note with reference to Alvis Cars and my own car (Chassis No. 1307) in particular? Perhaps you may recall that the car I have is the car which Mr. Harvey drove in the Scottish Light Car Trial last June. It was then that my attention was drawn to the Alvis, and since it has been in my possession my regard for it has increased fivefold.

As you can well imagine, I have more opportunity than most people for "trying out" cars of different makes. For all-round performance I have been in no car of similar horse-power which I would care to have in exchange for my Alvis.

What has surprised and delighted me more than anything else is the fact that it appears to be impossible to overdrive it. When first I read in your book of instructions that the car could be driven all day if need be at from 40 to 45 m.p.h., I was frankly sceptical. I thought this sort of thing came under the category of cruelty to light cars.

During the last six weeks I have driven my car at from 40 to 45 m.p.h. for hours at a stretch, and just to find out whether this treatment had made any difference, I tried the car "all out" on a main road (gradient about 1 in 12) yesterday, and the speedometer registered 48 m.p.h. on third gear!

Last week in Scotland was held the Six Days Reliability Trial for motor cycles, and I think I am safe in saying that a more strenuous route has never been included in a trial.

As an official knowing full well the difficulties to be encountered, I hesitated before deciding to go round on my Alvis. In the end I decided that it would be an excellent test for the car. I covered 1,019 miles during the week without experiencing the slightest trouble. I can give the car no better testimonial than to say that it ran faultlessly.

Incidentally, the car has now covered about 19,000 miles, and the only time I have been held up on the road was three weeks ago, when the magneto condenser gave out.

Yours faithfully,
Harold J. Cunningham.
Motoring Correspondent.

12-40 h.p. ALVIS
FOUR - SEATER
STANDARD MODEL

£430

Nine other Models from
£397.

May we send you a Catalogue and full particulars post free?

ALVIS CAR
& ENGINEERING CO., Ltd.,
COVENTRY.

Agents and Service Depots everywhere.

H.P.

Nearly 200 ALVIS CARS ALL-OUT AT BROOKLANDS—

AN EVENT UNIQUE IN MOTORING HISTORY.

DURING the past season ALVIS Cars have practically swept the board at all noteworthy competitions Success upon success has been piled up by private owners in all parts of the country for speed hill climbing and general reliability, gaining over 200 gold medals, cups and premier awards. On June 17th last the Annual ALVIS Brooklands Rally was held in order to give ALVIS owners an opportunity of testing their cars, of meeting each other and exchanging their experiences. A praiseworthy and courageous undertaking on the part of any motor manufacturer—convincing evidence of the confidence of the Alvis Company in its productions. Nearly 200 ALVIS Cars were tried all-out on the track, old and new, tuned and untuned, yet not a single breakdown occurred, nor did any car give the slightest trouble. Speeds of well over 60 miles per hour were common, and the premier award for well kept condition went to an ALVIS with over 30,000 miles to its credit. What a remarkable testimony to the reliability of ALVIS Cars. How many other makes would stand this test? The ALVIS is a car in a class by itself.

Quality alone in relation to price determines the true value of any car. Judged on the basis of quality the ALVIS must be admitted to stand supreme amongst the world's best cars. Built like a battleship, accurate, tested—built to endure, it marks the pinnacle of British engineering superiority. There is not only proved quality—but an air of quality about the ALVIS, circumstantial evidence about its owner, the one a compliment to the other. The ALVIS is essentially "The Car for the Connoisseur"—the man of experience who can appreciate the difference. There is a difference between the ALVIS and most other cars—the only way to appreciate the difference is to drive in an ALVIS.

Full Range of Models from £397.

Write for the name of the nearest Agent to you, who will be pleased to give you full particulars and a trial run,

The ALVIS CAR & ENGINEERING CO. LTD., COVENTRY.

"THE CAR FOR THE CONNOISSEUR"

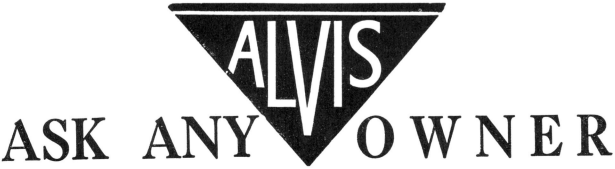

ASK ANY OWNER

H.P.
15

If you missed the

ALVIS

BRITISH
& BEST

You missed the MASTERPIECE OF THE SHOW

The famous British winner of the International 200 miles light car race at Brooklands, 13th October, 1923, at an average speed of **93·29** m.p.h.

ALVIS CAR & ENGINEERING CO. LTD., COVENTRY.

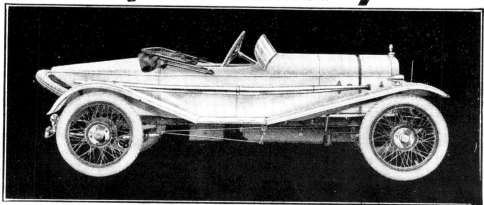
APRIL 1924

H.P.
17

Exchange your car for an ALVIS

"AND GET SATISFACTION

says Henlys Chief.

BECAUSE I will give you an astonishing price for your old car—and the Alvis will give you a measure of satisfaction you cannot get from any other car of its type.

For a £12 tax the Alvis provides 50 h.p.; on top gear she rides without snatching at 6 to 7 m.p.h., and in one effortless flash accelerates to 60 or 70 m.p.h. when desired.

Mr. John Prioleau, the famous motoring expert, said of the Alvis in the "Daily Mirror," of March 5th: "An outstandingly alluring car—fit, I should say, to go anywhere where roads exist and to keep on doing it. A real feather in the cap of the British Industry."

Such a testimony from such a critic is more than you or anyone can afford to ignore

Four examples of the magnificent range of Alvis cars, now in my Showrooms, are illustrated on this page. The prices range from £485 to £695, and every Alvis car is guaranteed for three years.

May I send you a catalogue?

It's an Alvis you want—and

Henlys *have it*

LONDON DISTRIBUTORS FOR ALVIS

Alvis Superiority—

ALVIS Superiority is talked about wherever Motorists meet, and no make of Car to-day has such a retinue of Enthusiastic Owners or Admirers.

Its Performance and Perfection are so pronounced that even "Runabout," that most critical contributor to "*The Autocar*," said, in the issue of the 4th July, that "IT WAS A ROAD CAR DE LUXE SUCH AS HE DID NOT EXPECT TO SEE FOR TEN YEARS TO COME."

The sheer delight of driving or riding in an ALVIS must be experienced to be appreciated. It is truly "The Car for the Connoisseur," and the demand for it has for many months exceeded the production. Make sure your next car is an ALVIS!

Write for Catalogue and nearest Agent's name and address.

THE ALVIS CAR & ENGINEERING CO., LTD., COVENTRY.

LONDON DISTRIBUTORS:—Henly's Ltd.,
91 & 155 Great Portland Street, W.1.

STANDARD MODEL	
12/40 h.p. 3-Seater	£397
DE LUXE MODELS	
12/40 h.p. 3-Seater	£475
With 12/50 h.p. O.H.V. Super Sports Engine extra	£75
12/40 h.p 4-Seater	£495
With 12/50 h.p. O.H.V. Super Sports Engine extra	£80
12/40 h.p. 5-Seater	£535
12/50 h.p. 2-Seater Super Sports O.H.V.	£550
12/50 h.p. 4-Seater Super Sports O.H.V.	£575
12/40 h.p. V-fronted 3 Seater Coupé	£575
12/40 h.p. 4 Seater Coupé Saloon	£650
12/40 h.p. 2/3-Seater V-fronted Saloon	£595
12/40 h.p. 4-Seater V-fronted Saloon	£695

BRITISH EMPIRE EXHIBITION STAND No. 120.

The GOLD CUP awarded to the ALVIS as WINNER of the 200 Miles INTERNATIONAL LIGHT CAR RACE, Brooklands, Oct., 1923, at an average speed of 93.29 m.p.h.

ALVIS

12/50 h.p. Four-Seater Super Sports, O.H.V. £575

H.P.

"The Car for the Connoisseur"

ALVIS

THE ALVIS BRINGS A NEW DELIGHT TO MOTORING

No matter how blasé to motoring you may have become, either from long experience or from weariness of the failings of many cars, the possession of an ALVIS will immediately bring a new delight. The difference, the immense superiority of the ALVIS will strike you the minute you take the wheel. Its wonderful responsiveness will echo every mood. A whim for speed and a touch of the accelerator will give you 60 m.p.h. or over. A mood for pottering and you can crawl along as slow as 5 m.p.h. without changing down. All the time you are conscious of delightful comfort. Silence, freedom from draught, and ease of comfort are synonymous with the word ALVIS. Try one for yourself to appreciate to the full this new delight. Any ALVIS agent will be pleased to arrange a trial run.

SEE ALVIS 1925 MODELS.

STAND SCOTTISH MOTOR SHOW. **22**

Write for fully illustrated catalogue and address of nearest agent.

THE ALVIS CAR & ENGINEERING CO., LTD., COVENTRY.

LONDON DISTRIBUTORS, Henly's Ltd., 91 & 155, Gt. Portland Street, W.1

39 RECORDS IN ONE RUN.

On Oct. 22nd Major C.M. Harvey driving an ALVIS Car broke all Brooklands Class A Records from $\frac{1}{2}$ mile up to 10 hours in 8 hours, achieving at times a lap speed of 96·9 m.p.h., and maintaining for the whole distance an average speed of 88 m.p.h. The most wonderful performance of the season.

H.P

20

NOVEMBER 1924

A REPUTATION THAT IS SUPREME

ALVIS Reputation is unassailable. . . . It has been built upon startling track and road performances . . . matured on unfailing service in the hands of regular motorists . . . and established upon the sound foundation of magnificent quality. . . . The World of Automobilism acknowledges Alvis to be supreme in all that makes motoring an undiluted joy.

Whether you choose the "Famous Four" or the "Supreme Six" the Alvis reputation is your guarantee. The Alvis Catalogue shows them to you in full colours. . . . Send for your copy.

THE ALVIS CAR AND ENGINEERING Co., Ltd., COVENTRY.
London Distributors: HENLYS, LTD,, Devonshire House, Piccadilly, and Gt, Portland Street, W.1.

WITH FIRST PUBLIC EXHIBITION OF THE
AMAZING FRONT WHEEL
DRIVE

Special opening events for this week only · · ·

Photo by Permission of " The Autocar"

Yesterday at 3 o'clock the curtain was raised on the most remarkable motor of all time—set in the largest motor Showroom in Europe, This exhibition and the celebrations which have marked the opening of Henly House continue for one week and are of the greatest interest to all motorists, for here is a car which has come to stay—to revolutionise motoring. To make travel faster yet safer and more comfortable than ever before.

Driven through the front wheels—each wheel separately sprung—centre of gravity lowest by far—these are three of the many features which will not fail to interest you.

In addition you will see at the new Henly House, a dazzling selection of cars, coachwork and colour schemes. Each of the seven floors contains different makes and types and in the basement there is a large array of used cars—available at extraordinary bargain prices for the opening week only. Henlys already famous terms are available for any car purchased and the highest possible prices are offered for cars in exchange. The wonderful guarantee policy in black and white for all used cars over £100 which has made such a sensation in the motoring world is for your benefit. This guarantee makes car purchase as safe and simple as buying a box of cigarettes.

"This week at Henlys" therefore is something you must on no account miss. *Pay a visit to-day.*

HENLYS

Henly House, 385-7, Euston Road, N.W.1 (opposite Gt. Portland Street Station). Phones: Museum 7734/9.

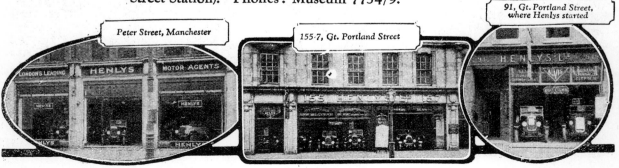

Peter Street, Manchester

155-7, Gt. Portland Street

91, Gt. Portland Street, where Henlys started

"Absolutely nothing to compare with it"....

—Says *Henlys' Chief*

Yes, I emphasise this fact!

Study Alvis feature by feature and you will find it "in a class by itself." Endeavour to emulate Alvis performance with any other car of like rating, whether 4 or 6 cylinder and you will be sadly disappointed.

Let us deal for one moment with the running costs of the Alvis 4-cylinder— Tax £12, but with development up to 50 h.p. Its consumption is 30 m.p.g. with a speed of anything up to 70 m.p.h. Tyres and oil costs correspondingly low, and the makers' guarantee of 3 years should be sufficient proof that repair costs form a negligible quantity. Where is there another car that can compare with this?

Alvis is *exclusive* in the true sense of the term. Each chassis is an individual masterpiece of mechanical construction, built for those who would enjoy to the full a new motoring sensation which was once only dreamed of, but which Alvis has made possible 10 years ahead of its time. This is not my thought but that of an authority on motoring and car construction.

At Henly house we have a whole floor devoted solely to Alvis models. Here you can also see the front wheel drive Alvis, that mechanical wizard which has created such world-wide interest. The colour schemes and luxurious coachwork are a sheer delight, and I invite you to pay a visit and indulge in the pleasure of a trial run at our expense.

* * *

The next best thing to a new Alvis is one of Henlys guaranteed used models. Full lists and particulars sent free on application. Call, phone or write to-day.

Front Wheel Drive Sports Saloon

6-cylinder—6 light 4-door Alvista Saloon

4-cylinder Sports Saloon

HENLYS

Sole ALVIS DISTRIBUTORS FOR LONDON & MANCHESTER

HENLY HOUSE, (Opposite Great Portland Street Station) 385-7, EUSTON ROAD, N.W.1   Phones: Museum 7734/9

DEVONSHIRE HOUSE, PICCADILLY.   91, 155-157, GT. PORTLAND ST., W.1.
1, 3 & 5, PETER ST., MANCHESTER. Phone: Central 1780.   London Service Station : HAWLEY CRESCENT, CAMDEN TOWN.
Hampstead 5177.

THEY'RE RIGHT INSIDE THE INNER CIRCLE

Not mass but class production cars, built up to a standard—not down to a price—that's the ALVIS, the finest medium-powered car ever made.

But there's no need to take our word for it—try one at our expense so that you can judge for yourself.

The models include:

12/75 h.p. Front wheel drive		
2-str. Sports		£597
4-str. Sports		£597
4-str. Sports Saloon ...		£650
12/50 h.p. 4-cyl. 2/3 str. ...		£485
4-cyl. 4/5 str. ...		£495
4-cyl. Alvista Flexible Saloon ...		£595
"Atlantic" Coachbuilt Saloon		£595
14/75 h.p. 6-cyl. models as 4-cyl. models but £100 extra.		

ALVIS

HENLYS

ENGLAND'S LEADING MOTOR AGENTS'

12/50 h.p. 4 cylr.
Alvista Saloon £595

ALVIS

12/75 h.p. Front
Wheel Drive Super
Charged 2 Seater
£625

14/75 h.p. 6 cylr.
Coachbuilt Saloon
£695

12/75 h.p. Front
Wheel Drive Super
Charged 4 Seater
£625

14/75 h.p. Alvista
6 Light Saloon £695

AMAZING RANGE OF MODELS AT STAND No. 38

COACHWORK to suit all needs—and fascinate even the most fastidious — plus the finest medium-powered chassis ever made — that's what Alvis represents—that's why you must not miss it at Olympia.

There are the astounding new Front Wheel Drive models—the 14/75 h.p. 6-cylr. Long chassis, and the world-famous 12/50 h.p. 4-cylr. Short chassis.

Five striking examples will be on the Alvis Stand No. 38, and a further selection at Henlys' Depot just opposite Olympia. Incidentally, this depot has been specially taken to assist Alvis and Henly customers. Leave your coats and parcels there. Make your appointments. Use it to the utmost—there is no obligation : just an honest endeavour to give you a better and higher standard of service than is obtainable elsewhere.

Above all, get Henlys' price for your car in exchange, and get the benefit of Henlys' terms and vast facilities. It will pay you over and over again to buy your car from

HENLYS

For nine years the Alvis "Famous Four" has held an unassailable reputation in the Automobile world . . . Today it is the acknowledged leader in its class . . a magnificent engineering production . . a supreme car.

ALVIS CAR & ENGINEERING CO., LTD., COVENTRY.

London Distributors: HENLYS LTD. HENLY HOUSE, EUSTON RD. N.W.

ALVIS

IF you seek a superlative car "under 1,500 c.c." you will choose the Alvis "Famous Four"... a car that for eight years has been acknowledged the greatest engineering achievement in its class.

There is in the Alvis range a car that will exceed your greatest expectations . . . and give you motoring joy in its fullest sense . . . Send for the Alvis catalogue . . . and discover Alvis supremacy . . .

ALVIS CAR & ENGINEERING CO., LIMITED, COVENTRY.

London Distributors: HENLYS LTD. HENLY HOUSE, EUSTON ROAD. N.W.

Never has the reputation of Alvis cars stood so high as to-day ... Never in the history of the Alvis Company has the name represented such outstanding car value and so great an advance beyond contemporary effort. The Alvis car of to-day fulfils the greatest ambition of its manufacturers—to produce a car superlative in every detail. The All-British Alvis is worthy of your earnest study before you buy your 1930 car.

ALVIS CAR & ENGINEERING CO. LIMITED, COVENTRY.

London Distributors: HENLYS LTD., PICCADILLY and EUSTON ROAD, N.W.

The 1931 Policy

# of ALVIS

THE famous Alvis " Silver Eagle," built to meet the demand of the connoisseur of matters motoring, and an entirely new model in the Alvis " Twelve-Fifty." . . . In these two cars—each the highest attainment in its class—the Alvis Company will meet all the needs of the discerning motorist. See these famous cars at the Showrooms of your local Alvis Distributor or Agent.

ALVIS CAR & ENGINEERING CO., LTD., COVENTRY.

London Distributors: Henlys Ltd., Piccadilly and Euston Road, N.W.

There are 150 leading Agents throughout London and the Provinces who will be delighted to demonstrate ALVIS superiority, or, if you prefer, we will gladly arrange for one of our factory representatives to visit you personally

DUNLOP TYRES STANDARD.

master of the king's highway

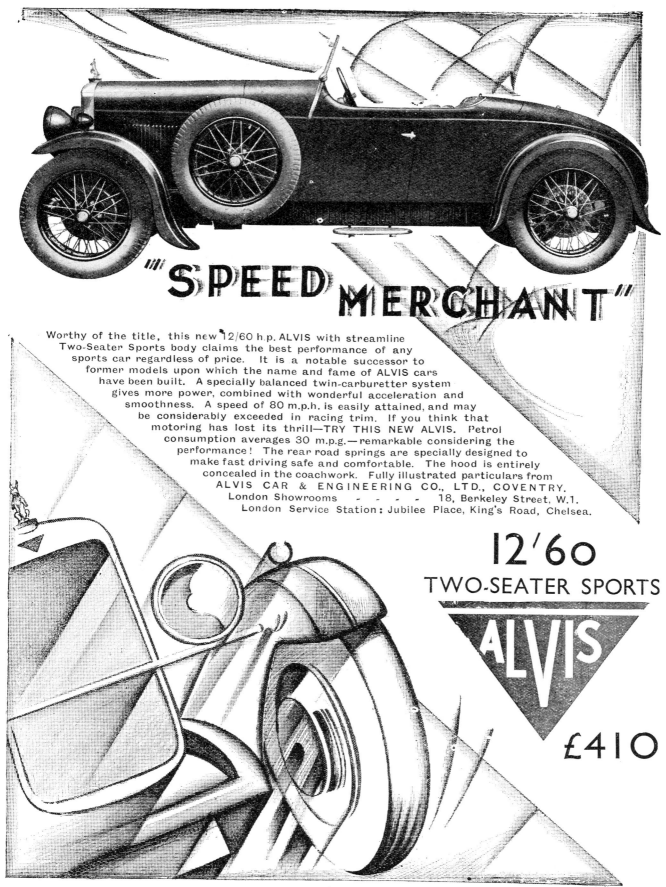

"SPEED MERCHANT"

Worthy of the title, this new 12/60 h.p. ALVIS with streamline Two-Seater Sports body claims the best performance of any sports car regardless of price. It is a notable successor to former models upon which the name and fame of ALVIS cars have been built. A specially balanced twin-carburetter system gives more power, combined with wonderful acceleration and smoothness. A speed of 80 m.p.h. is easily attained, and may be considerably exceeded in racing trim. If you think that motoring has lost its thrill—TRY THIS NEW ALVIS. Petrol consumption averages 30 m.p.g.—remarkable considering the performance! The rear road springs are specially designed to make fast driving safe and comfortable. The hood is entirely concealed in the coachwork. Fully illustrated particulars from
ALVIS CAR & ENGINEERING CO., LTD., COVENTRY.
London Showrooms - - - - 18, Berkeley Street, W.1.
London Service Station: Jubilee Place, King's Road, Chelsea.

12'60
TWO-SEATER SPORTS
ALVIS
£410

A MAGNIFICENT RANGE OF QUALITY CARS **AL**

NOW almost the same price as ordinary cars, but so much better in quality and performance—the all-British ALVIS represents the most advanced design in automobile practice

12/60 h.p. 2-seater Sports, £450

As a result of twelve years' concentration on making nothing but the best, the incorporation of many exclusive features and patents, and the experience gained in classic trials and speed events—the ALVIS Car is unequalled in speed, safety, riding comfort, and economy in service.

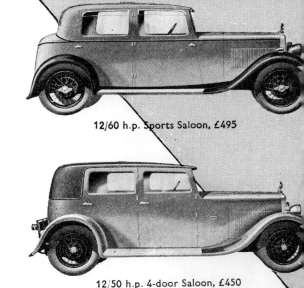

12/60 h.p. Sports Saloon, £495

12/50 h.p. 4-door Saloon, £450

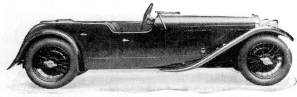

"Speed Twenty" 4-seater Sports, £695

DRIVE AN ALVIS AND REDISCOVER TH

Choose an **ALVIS** prices fro

"MASTER OF THE

VIS PRICES FROM £395 —A MODEL FOR EVERY MOTORIST

20 h.p. "Mayfair" Four Light Saloon, £775

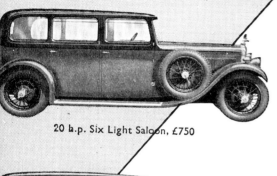

20 h.p. Six Light Saloon, £750

20 h.p. "Mayfair" Limousine, £795

Y OF MOTORING

"SPEED TWENTY" "SILVER EAGLE" 12/60 & 12/50 MODELS

"Atlantic" Saloon, 16·95 h.p., £695   20 h.p., £750

At prices from £395 ALVIS OFFERS TRUE ECONOMY

—to pay less is a compromise with quality

It is a true saying that "Quality is the best economy "—but never more so than in the purchase of a motor car. It is impossible by mass-production methods to build into a car such qualities as are exclusive to the ALVIS

Many experienced motorists recognise this, and make the ALVIS their final choice after a long process of elimination. Is it not wisest to pay from £395 for an ALVIS Car and get these super-qualities without further delay?

There is an ALVIS Model to suit your individual requirements—choose from this complete range of smart cars. Illustrated particulars and demonstrations from

ALVIS CAR AND ENGINEERING CO. LTD., COVENTRY.
London Showrooms: 18, Berkeley Street, W.1

£395

KING'S HIGHWAY"

ALVIS Silver Eagle

THE ALVIS "Silver Eagle" is quite different from any other car that you can buy. Consider these definite facts:

The ALVIS "Silver Eagle" is built for speed, but also to be safe, silent, flexible, and superlatively comfortable under all conditions.

NOV. 11 REMEMBRANCE DAY GIVE GENEROUSLY FOR YOUR POPPY

The ALVIS "Silver Eagle" is designed to give years of unfailing service, and when replacements or repairs eventually are required, each wearing part can be renewed or adjusted individually at low cost.

ALVIS "Silver Eagle" bodywork is by England's leading Coach-builders . . . . roomy, restful and beautiful of line.

ALVIS leadership in automobile design has never yet been challenged. Own an ALVIS, Master of the King's Highway.

ALVIS CAR & ENGINEERING COMPANY LTD., COVENTRY.
LONDON SHOWROOMS:
18, Berkeley Street, W.1.

"Firefly Twelve" from £455

"Silver Eagle" from £585

"Speed Twenty" from £695

20h.p. "Silver Eagle" Mayfair 4-light Saloon.... £775

Choose an
ALVIS *for* 1933!

"Firefly Twelve" *from* £455
"Silver Eagle" *from* £695
"Speed Twenty" *from* £695

Each car the Leader of its Class. See them at

OLYMPIA
Stand 56 Main Hall

WHETHER you desire a speedy sports car or a luxurious limousine, four cylinders or six, your choice should be an ALVIS, leader of its class.

The genius of ALVIS design, the fine workmanship of skilled craftsmen, have carried the fame of ALVIS throughout the world. Discriminating motorists find in the ALVIS incomparable performance allied with long life and low running costs .... a grace of appearance and refinement of control possessed by no other car.

Yet each ALVIS model costs much less than you would expect to pay for such outstanding quality. Take the first step towards better motoring by writing for full particulars to

ALVIS CAR & ENGINEERING COMPANY LTD., COVENTRY.

FIREFLY · Speed Twenty · Silver Eagle

"MASTERS OF THE KINGS HIGHWAY"

OCTOBER 1932

ALVIS 20 h.p. "SILVER EAGLE" 7-SEATED LIMOUSINE £795

A LUXURY CAR of irreproachable manners and high performance, the ALVIS "SILVER EAGLE"

is definitely quite different from any other car you can buy. Consider these unique points:

The ALVIS "Silver Eagle" is built for speed, but also to be safe, silent, flexible, and superlatively comfortable under all conditions. It has beauty of appearance in harmony with its mechanical perfection.

The ALVIS "Silver Eagle" is designed to give years of unfailing service, and when replacements or repairs eventually are required, each wearing part can be renewed or adjusted individually at low cost.

SCOTTISH
MOTOR
SHOW
Stands
29
30
12

ALVIS "Silver Eagle" bodywork is by England's leading Coachbuilders . . . roomy, restful and beautiful of line.

ALVIS leadership in automobile design has never yet been challenged. Own an ALVIS, and enjoy many years of perfect motoring.

ALVIS CAR & ENGINEERING
COMPANY, LIMITED,
COVENTRY.
London Showrooms:
18, Berkeley
Street,
W.1

ALVIS
"Firefly
Twelve"
from £455
"Speed
Twenty"
from £695

from £585

NOVEMBER 1932

ALVIS

Charles Follett invites you to take the wheel of the Speed 20 ALVIS.

With Van den Plas sports 4-seater
£725

You take fierce acceleration—high speeds for granted in any good sports car. But how many are really docile in traffic? Can crawl without snatch, on top?

Every Speed Twenty Alvis can!

You take smart streamlined bodies for granted on expensive sports cars. But how many are really comfortable? Untiring on long runs?

Every Speed Twenty Alvis is!

To prove these facts you must take the wheel yourself. Only then can you appreciate the care and thought put into these magnificent cars.

Test, under everyday road conditions, the fast cornering in safety — dead accurate steering—smooth road holding.

Experience its fierce acceleration—speeds as high as roads permit — brakes that will grapple with any emergency.

You will then realise why the Speed Twenty Alvis puts up such high averages in such an effortless manner.

But come along to Berkeley Street, and drive one yourself.

• with special coachwork obtainable from

Charles Follett Ltd
[Sole Distributors for ALVIS in London & District]

MAYFAIR 6266

18, Berkeley St, London, W.1.

BERKELEY
COACHWORK

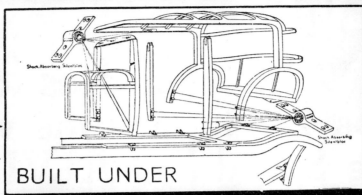

BUILT UNDER

SILENT TRAVEL PATENTS

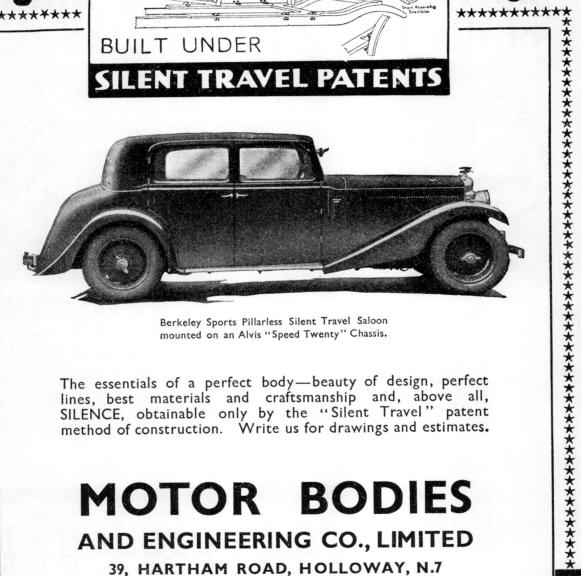

Berkeley Sports Pillarless Silent Travel Saloon
mounted on an Alvis "Speed Twenty" Chassis.

The essentials of a perfect body—beauty of design, perfect
lines, best materials and craftsmanship and, above all,
SILENCE, obtainable only by the "Silent Travel" patent
method of construction. Write us for drawings and estimates.

MOTOR BODIES
AND ENGINEERING CO., LIMITED
39, HARTHAM ROAD, HOLLOWAY, N.7
'Phone: NORTH 5407-8

OCTOBER 1933

The "FIREFLY TWELVE"

ALVIS

...the Most Luxurious Car in the Economy Class!

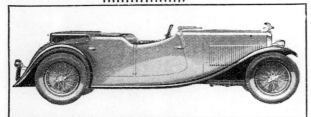

THE SPORTS FOUR-SEATER - - £475

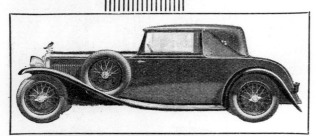

THE 4-SEATER DROPHEAD COUPE £495

YOU will be amazed that a car of only twelve h.p. rating can give such brilliant performance . . . such ample accommodation and refinement of comfort . . . so many features hitherto associated with cars far larger and more costly.

The Wilson Pre-selective Gearbox—£15 extra in all models—even enhances this fine performance. A movement of the neat lever below the steering wheel, made at leisure; a pressure of the gear pedal, and you have changed gear— instantly, noiselessly, with vivid acceleration now at your command.

Let us make an appointment for you to drive this fine car !

ALVIS CAR & ENG. COMPANY, LTD., COVENTRY.

SALOON, with Sliding Roof ... £495

FACILITATE BUSINESS, and ensure prompt attention to your enquiries, by mentioning "THE LIGHT CAR" when writing to advertisers. They will appreciate it.

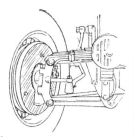

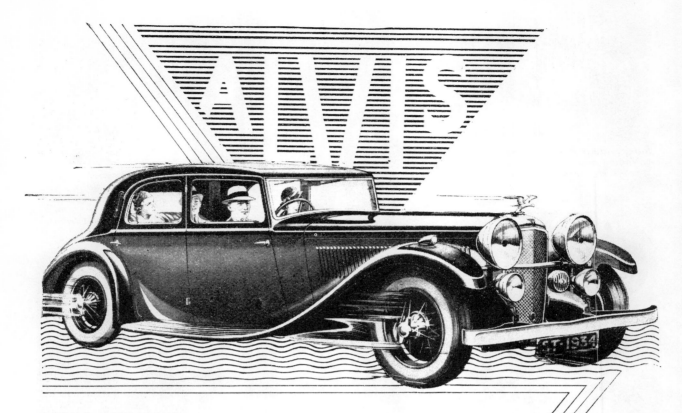

ROUGH ROADS DO NOT EXIST

The riding comfort in ALVIS "Speed Twenty" and "Crested Eagle" Models must be experienced to be believed. Each front wheel is independently sprung and steered, and it is impossible for road shocks to be communicated to the steering, so that even when the surface is extremely rough, high speeds can be indulged in with perfect stability and safety. ALVIS have led the way in British automobile design by producing and perfecting this system of suspension during the past six years. Now, it is being offered by the leading Continental and American car manufacturers as *"the latest advance in automobile practice."* To keep up-to-date, choose an ALVIS!

There are 1934 Models from £475.   Full particulars from
ALVIS CAR & ENGINEERING CO., LTD., COVENTRY

INDEPENDENT FRONT WHEEL SPRINGING & STEERING

H.P.

MODERN MOTORING
demands the elimination of all driving fatigue

RIGID hands, tense muscles, tired eyes and fatigue due to long-distance driving over rough roads are entirely eliminated by the unique ALVIS system of INDEPENDENT FRONT WHEEL SPRINGING AND STEERING, which counteracts all road shocks even at high speeds. In production over six years ago, this is no untried feature, but a proved development in automobile design now being adopted by the leading Continental and American car manufacturers. The ALL-BRITISH ALVIS always leads the way.

As incorporated in " Crested Eagle" Models from £750, and " Speed Twenty" Models from £695. Other models from £475. May we send details?

ALVIS CAR & ENGINEERING CO., LTD., COVENTRY.

London Showrooms : 18, Berkeley Street, W.1.
London Service Station : Jubilee Place, King's Road, Chelsea, S.W.3.

Independent Front Wheel Springing and Steering exclusive to ALVIS

ALVIS

"CRESTED EAGLE"
"SPEED TWENTY"

H.P.

ALVIVACITY -

motoring's greatest joy –

may now be indulged in through the medium of the "SIXTEEN" ALVIS, a new Model incorporating all the best features of the "Firefly Twelve" and many of the famous "Speed Twenty." It offers at a price which at once appeals to one's sense of value, all those outstanding qualities which have made the all-British ALVIS famous throughout the world. In all-round motoring value this ALVIS challenges comparison. The six-cylinder engine, rated at 16.95 h.p., develops a speed in excess of seventy miles an hour, whilst the all-synchromesh four-speed gearbox (an exclusive ALVIS feature) makes gear changing swift, silent, and certain. Brilliant performance on the road, ample and comfortable seating accommodation, and coachwork of super excellence characterise this new Model. May we send you fully illustrated particulars and arrange a demonstration ?

ALVIS CAR & ENGINEERING COMPANY, LTD., COVENTRY.

London Showrooms : 18, Berkeley Street, W.1.   London Service Station : Jubilee Place, King's Road, Chelsea, S.W.3.

Economically obtainable in the
NEW SIXTEEN

ALVIS

| ALL SYNCHRO MESH ALL SILENT 4 SPEED GEARBOX *The only one in production* | ALVIS PATENT SELF-SERVO BRAKES · CENTRAL BRAKE ADJUSTMENT *from Drivers Seat* | LOW CHASSIS WITH FULLY FLOATING REAR AXLE · *Speed in excess of 70 m.p.h* |

Introduced since the Olympia Motor Show
PRICE £595

H.P.

ALVIVACITY -

the thrill of driving an ALVIS

ıs an unforgettable experience which brings relief from the commonplace. The joyous response to every mood, vivid acceleration without a tremor of vibration, speed in smoothness and silence, perfect suspension and ease of control . . . . these are exclusive ALVIS features best expressed by the word "ALVIVACITY." Independent front wheel springing and steering, the latest advance in automobile practice, has been in production on ALVIS cars for the past six years, and is incorporated in all "Crested Eagle" and "Speed Twenty" Models. There is a wide choice of 1934 ALVIS Cars from £475. May we send you illustrated particulars and arrange a demonstration?

ALVIS CAR & ENGINEERING Co. Ltd., COVENTRY

London Showrooms : 18 Berkeley Street, W.1.   London Service Station : Jubilee Place, King's Road, S.W.3.

"SPEED 20"

H.P.

The Car of the Moment

Above is a four-seater drop-head coupe on the Speed Twenty chassis with coachwork specially built to the design of Charles Follett. This car is equipped with 4-speed synchromesh gearbox, independent front wheel springing and steering and has an exceptionally brilliant performance on the road.

Price **£885**

The Crested Eagle four light Saloon (centre) has pre-selective self-change 4-speed gears, independent front wheel suspension and steering and a host of other fascinating features that make this car ideal for town or long distance touring

Price **£750**

Those who require a car capable of averaging high speeds combined with the docility of a town carriage should investigate the wonderful capabilities of the New Alvis 16 shown below. This car incorporates synchromesh silent 4-speed gearbox and every up-to-the-minute feature of 1934 motoring.

Six light Saloon. Price **£595**

All the above models and many more can be seen at 18, Berkeley Street, the London home of Alvis cars. Any car will be gladly placed at your disposal without obligation.

ALVIS

Sole Distributors for Alvis in London and Home Counties.

Charles Follett, Ltd.
18, BERKELEY STREET, W.1.
PHONE: MAYFAIR 6266
LONDON SERVICE STATION, JUBILEE PLACE, KINGS ROAD, S.W.

4 Distinguished Models for 1935

ALVIS

The NEW "Speed Twenty"
The NEW "Silver Eagle"
The NEW "Firebird"
and the famous
"Crested Eagle"

A Statement of Policy

The ALVIS policy of making nothing but the best, and by constant research and experiment maintaining a lead in automobile design, has resulted in a line of thoroughbred cars whose performance has been unsurpassed during the past fifteen years.

The ALVIS 1935 Programme continues this policy in a particularly virile form. To the well-proved exclusive ALVIS features, such as independent springing and steering, all synchro-mesh gearbox, etc., have been added many improvements. Three entirely new engines develop increased power with a silence and a degree of smoothness hitherto unobtainable. Improved chassis construction results in better suspension, greater road clearance, and many refinements. Coachwork of new design with an improved method of mounting makes for added beauty and long trouble-free life.

ALVIS 1935 Models combine ALVIS high speed performance with beauty, comfort, and safety in a considerably enhanced degree. The ALVIS Company, proud of its achievements in the past, offers the 1935 Models with full confidence in their outstanding merits.

T.G. John.

Managing Director.

ALVIS CAR & ENGINEERING CO. LTD. COVENTRY

49

"ALVIVACITY."... even

ALVIS

The NEW "Speed Twenty"

THE most dignified fast car you can buy, with every refinement conducive to silence and comfort. Exceptional smoothness of running, unlimited braking power, effortless steering, and a unique system of suspension combine to present the fascination of motoring in an ALVIS at its zenith. Peak performance with every modern improvement. This is an entirely NEW "Speed Twenty" Model. The new six-cylinder engine, 19.82 h.p. produces still more power without any sacrifice of flexibility, and with smoothness and silence definitely enhanced. The new chassis frame is braced at every point to give balanced rigidity throughout its length. Rear suspension embodies the advantages of both underslung and overslung principles, and the road-holding qualities are exceptionally efficient. The unique ALVIS system of independent front-wheel steering and springing has been so perfected as to absorb all road shocks, and driving strain even on long journeys is entirely eliminated. Another important feature is the all-silent all-synchromesh four-speed gearbox, the efficiency of which has been proved by many ALVIS owners during the past year. In beauty and grace of coachwork, a degree of excellence has been evolved to give the utmost comfort to the passengers. Visibility has been especially studied; there are no "blind" spots, and leg and head room are unusually generous. All "Speed Twenty" Models are provided with enclosed luggage containers of ample proportions, and the permanent jacking system is another feature of special interest to owner-drivers. For full specification, please write for 1935 "Speed Twenty" Brochure.

SPORTS SALOON	£850
4 STR. COUPÉ	£850
4 STR. SPORTS	£700
CHASSIS	£600

ALL EX WORKS

The well proved "Crested

So impressed have experienced motorists been with this wonderful car, whose every feature is planned for super-efficient service and long life, that no change is considered necessary for 1935. The soundness of its design, the brilliance of its performance, and its proved reliability over thousands of miles have established an ALVIS reputation well-nigh unique. This most brilliant example of advanced engineering practice,

more fascinating than before

The NEW "Silver Eagle"

ALVIS

FAST, safe, and easy to drive, this all-purpose car is generously proportioned, affording luxurious and roomy accommodation to all passengers. The 1935 "Silver Eagle" is an entirely new Model, with a six-cylinder engine, rated at 16.95 h.p., which provides silent, sustained speed, with the flexibility demanded by modern road conditions. It incorporates many new and unique ALVIS features, including the patent all-silent all-synchromesh four-speed gearbox. Effortless, silent changes up or down with certainty increase the pleasure of driving this powerful car. Low built to hold the road in comfort and safety, and with powerful self-energising brakes and Marles-Weller steering; long-distance driving may be undertaken with negligible effort. Coachwork is of the highest order, and every detail of interior finish and equipment will inspire a pride of ownership at all times. Best quality leather upholstery is used throughout, with deep pile carpets and burr walnut cabinet work, which give the interior the comfort and refinement usually associated with more costly cars. There is a choice of twelve body colours, and six shades for the upholstery. A full range of Models to suit all tastes, with closed, coupé, and open bodies of distinctive appearance should meet a popular demand for an all-purpose car of 16 h.p. with the ALVIS reputation for sound engineering and durability. For full specification, please write for 1935 "Silver Eagle" Brochure.

6 LIGHT SALOON	£598
4 LIGHT SALOON	£598
4 STR. COUPÉ	£598
4 STR. SPORTS	£585
CHASSIS	£485

ALL EX WORKS

Eagle" remains unchanged

with coachwork of imposing appearance and faultless finish has received the unqualified approval of connoisseurs of motoring who are satisfied only with the best. With 16.95 h.p. and 20 h.p. engines, the "Crested Eagle" offers a choice of horsepower from £750, and each Model incorporates the well-proved ALVIS system of independent front wheel springing and steering. For town or country use there is a Four-light Saloon, Six-light Saloon, and Seven-seater Limousine.

The NEW "Firebird"

ALVIS

N O other car gives such a performance at anywhere near the price as this new ALVIS Model. Developed from the well-known 12/50 Model, the new engine rated at 13.22 h.p. has an increased capacity which provides a much greater reserve of power, higher maximum speed and improved acceleration. Moderately rated, economical to run and maintain, it nevertheless possesses all those big-car features which are exclusive to ALVIS design. A big feature of the specification in a car so economically priced, is the inclusion of the ALVIS patent all-silent, all synchro-mesh four-speed gearbox, as fitted to the famous "Speed Twenty" Model. With this gearbox a greatly enhanced road performance is possible, and it is difficult to believe that a four-cylinder engine can produce such effortless power, such thrilling speed up to 75 m.p.h. with smoothness, comfort, and safety. Semi-elliptic springs of exceptional length, and scientific bracing of the new chassis frame contribute largely to the riding comfort and road-holding qualities at all speeds. Superb suspension, with Marles-Weller steering and ALVIS patent self-energising brakes ensures perfect control, and entirely eliminates driving strain even on the longest journey. The new fourteen horsepower "Firebird," with a host of exclusive ALVIS features unobtainable in any other car, offers all the fascination of driving an ALVIS at a remarkably low price. Examine the chassis and specification from stem to stern. Every component reflects the genius of ALVIS engineering. Coachwork is modern yet sensible, designed to give maximum visibility and comfort. Interior dimensions are unusually generous, and all controls are conveniently placed. With all bodies there is a choice of twelve colours, and six for the upholstery. For full specification, please write for 1935 "Firebird" Brochure.

4 LIGHT SALOON	£510
4 STR. COUPÉ	£510
4 STR. SPORTS	£490
CHASSIS	£410
ALL EX WORKS	

"ALVIVACITY" in its most economical form

Coachwork for the Connoisseur~

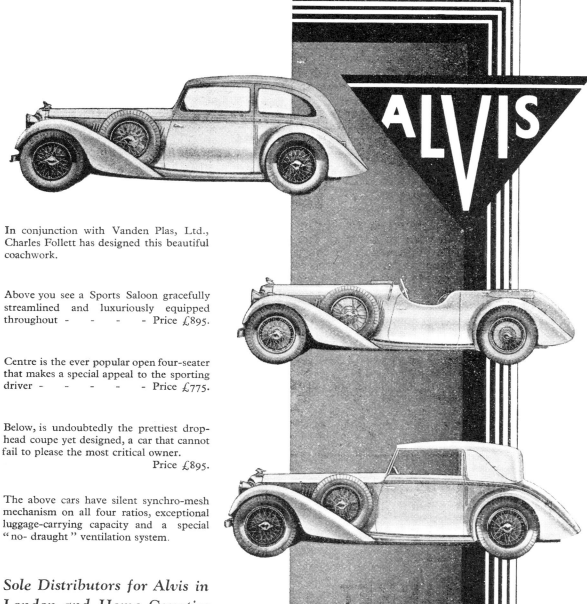

In conjunction with Vanden Plas, Ltd., Charles Follett has designed this beautiful coachwork.

Above you see a Sports Saloon gracefully streamlined and luxuriously equipped throughout -   -   -   - Price £895.

Centre is the ever popular open four-seater that makes a special appeal to the sporting driver -   -   -   - Price £775.

Below, is undoubtedly the prettiest drop-head coupe yet designed, a car that cannot fail to please the most critical owner.
Price £895.

The above cars have silent synchro-mesh mechanism on all four ratios, exceptional luggage-carrying capacity and a special " no- draught " ventilation system.

Sole Distributors for Alvis in London and Home Counties

CHARLES

FOLLETT *Ltd*
18, BERKELEY STREET, LONDON W.I.
PHONE: MAYFAIR 6266

LONDON SERVICE STATION : —
JUBILEE PLACE, KINGS ROAD, CHELSEA, S.W.

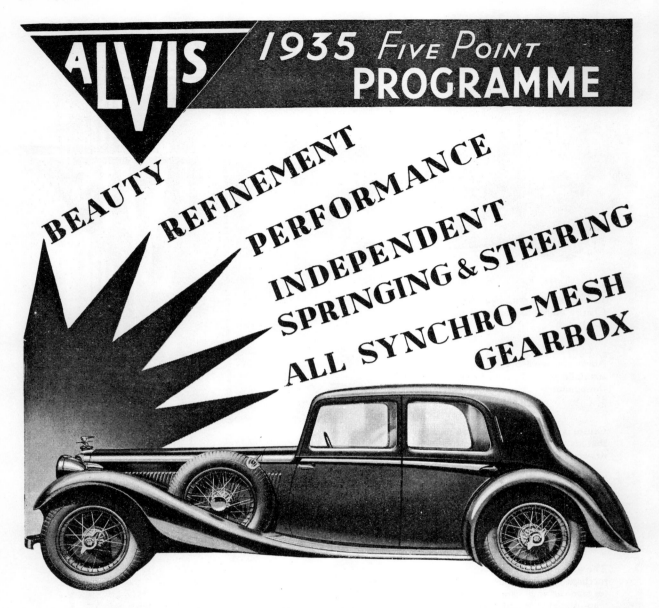

ALVIS 1935 FIVE POINT PROGRAMME

BEAUTY REFINEMENT PERFORMANCE INDEPENDENT SPRINGING & STEERING ALL SYNCHRO-MESH GEARBOX

1935 MODELS & PRICES

THE NEW 14 h.p. "FIREBIRD"

Four-Light Saloon	£510
Four-seater Coupe	£510
Four-seater Sports	£490

THE NEW 16 h.p. "SILVER EAGLE"

Six-Light Saloon	£598
Four-Light Saloon	£598
Four-seater Coupe	£598
Four-seater Sports	£585

THE NEW 20 h.p. "SPEED TWENTY"

Sports Saloon	£850
Four-seater Coupe	£850
Four-seater Sports	£700

16-95 h.p. and 20 h.p. "CRESTED EAGLE"

Four-Light Saloon	£750
Six-Light Saloon	£750
Seven-seater Limousine	£850

THE 1935 ALVIS is better than ever. To the many well-proved exclusive features have been added further refinements and improvements which make this thoroughbred car still more desirable. Three entirely new engines develop increased power with a silence and degree of smoothness hitherto unobtainable. New ideas in chassis construction, suspension, and coachwork all contribute towards the furtherance of an ideal in making nothing but the best. ALVIS performance, with every feature proved to enhance the pleasures of motoring, keeps the 1935 ALVIS in the forefront of the world's best cars. Before you buy your next car, see and try a new ALVIS. There is no substitute! 1935 Brochures for each Model are now available. ALVIS CAR & ENG. CO., LTD., COVENTRY.

London Showrooms: 18, Berkeley Street, W.1.

H.P.

ALVIS REPUTATION
is an asset you cannot obtain with any other car. It is unique!

FOR many years genius of design and superb workmanship have made the name of ALVIS famous throughout the world, indeed its leadership in these respects has never yet been challenged. Incomparable performance allied with luxurious comfort, long life and low running costs are characteristic features of this all-British car. Own an ALVIS, and time will but increase your pride in its possession. Of irreproachable quality and distinguished appearance, the ALVIS "Crested Eagle" offers to all discriminating motorists a superb motor car ranking equal with the world's best. From £750, its price is remarkably low in comparison with the high standard of motoring luxury it affords.

Of the many features incorporated to enhance the performance of the car, and the comfort of the passengers, special mention must be made of the exceptionally flexible six-cylinder engine, and the **INDEPENDENT FRONT WHEEL SPRINGING** and **STEERING**. This system of suspension has been in production on **ALVIS** cars for the past six years, and is therefore no experimental feature.

May we send you full particulars?

ALVIS CAR & ENGINEERING CO., LTD., COVENTRY.

London Showrooms : 18, Berkeley Street, W.1.
London Service Station : Jubilee Place, King's Road, S.W.3.

ALVIVACITY

H.P.

"CRESTED EAGLE"

"The Car for the Connoisseur"

The most dignified fast car you can buy

In the 1935 "Speed Twenty," ALVIS engineers have produced a car which brings a new dignity to fast motoring, and a new conception of silence and comfort at high speeds. The perfected ALVIS system of independent front wheel springing and steering, and the all-silent, all-synchromesh four speed gearbox, combined with luxurious passenger accommodation and superb coachwork, mark the new ALVIS "Speed Twenty" as definitely leading the world in automobile design. There is a full range of "Speed Twenty" Models with open or closed coachwork from £700. Other Models from £490. We shall be pleased to arrange demonstrations and supply fully illustrated particulars upon request.

ALVIS   CAR   &   ENGINEERING   COMPANY,   LTD.,   COVENTRY

London Service Station : Jubilee Place, King's Road, Chelsea, S.W.3

Distributors for London and Home Counties : Charles Follett, Ltd., 18, Berkeley Street, W.1

H.P.

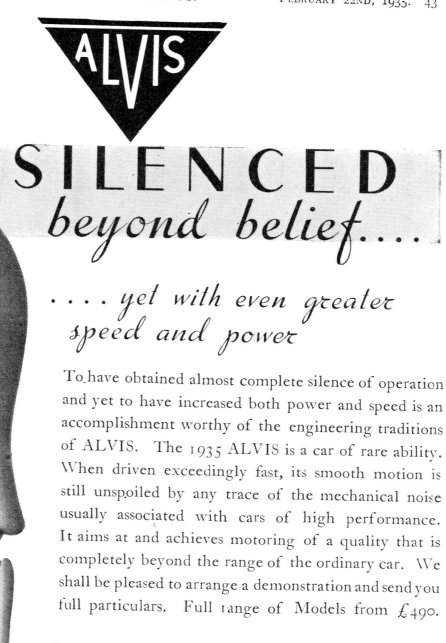

ALVIS

SILENCED
beyond belief.....

.... yet with even greater speed and power

To have obtained almost complete silence of operation and yet to have increased both power and speed is an accomplishment worthy of the engineering traditions of ALVIS. The 1935 ALVIS is a car of rare ability. When driven exceedingly fast, its smooth motion is still unspoiled by any trace of the mechanical noise usually associated with cars of high performance. It aims at and achieves motoring of a quality that is completely beyond the range of the ordinary car. We shall be pleased to arrange a demonstration and send you full particulars. Full range of Models from £490.

ALVIS CAR & ENGINEERING CO. LTD., COVENTRY
London Service Station : Jubilee Place, King's Road, Chelsea, S.W.3.
Distributors for London and Home Counties :
Charles Follett, Ltd., 18, Berkeley Street, W.1.

H.P.

The NEW CRESTED EAGLE

ALVIS

A MODERN MASTERPIECE

—the Motor Car for those who

appreciate quality & leadership

ALVIS, who have originated many of the most advanced features of modern automobile design, announce the new "CRESTED EAGLE."   In producing this new Model, ALVIS engineers have provided first and foremost a car of exceptional refinement and luxurious comfort, yet with these qualities they have successfully combined the true characteristics of ALVIS performance. The new "CRESTED EAGLE" is a worthy addition to the range of famous ALVIS Models, and a car which establishes an entirely new sense of motoring enjoyment.   Four Light Saloon £800, Special Six Light Saloon £800, Limousine £900.

ALVIS CAR & ENGINEERING CO. LTD., COVENTRY.   *London Service Station:—
Great West Road, Brentford.   Distributors for London and Home Counties: Charles Follett, Ltd., 18, Berkeley St., W.1*

THE CAR FOR THE CONNOISSEUR

The New "FIREBIRD"

NO OTHER CAR gives such performance at anywhere near the price. Economical to run and maintain, yet possessing all the exclusive features of ALVIS design, this new "FIREBIRD" Model will appeal to the many motorists who are familiar with the fame of ALVIS four-cylinder engines and their performance. Moderate in rating (Tax £10.10.0), with the all-silent, all-synchromesh four speed gearbox, Marles-Weller steering, and patent self-energising brakes, this Model offers "ALVIVACITY" at an extremely low figure, from **£490**. May we send you illustrated particulars?

ALVIS CAR & ENGINEERING COMPANY, LTD., COVENTRY
London Service Station : Great West Road, Brentford
Distributors for London & Home Counties :
Charles Follett, Ltd., 18, Berkeley Street, W.1

ALVIS

ALVIVACITY —
in its most economical form!

H.P.

15 YEARS OF POST-WAR PROGRESS

THE
**BLUE RIBAND
OF MOTORING**
200 Miles Race, Oct., 1923
In October, 1923, ALVIS won
for Britain the J.C.C. 200
MILES RACE at Brooklands,
in record time at an average
speed of 93.29 m.p.h.
*"Never was success more
deservedly attained."*
—THE AUTOCAR.

FROM 1920 to 1935 ALVIS engineers have steadfastly pursued the policy of making nothing but the best.

Experience gained in a wide programme of racing has been assiduously applied to expedite the evolution of the perfect high performance car. Acknowledged to be predominant in automobile design, ALVIS have produced :—

THE FIRST AND ONLY BRITISH CAR TO WIN THE J.C.C. 200 MILES RACE

THE FIRST BRITISH CAR WITH FLEXIBLE ENGINE AND GEARBOX MOUNTINGS

THE FIRST BRITISH CAR WITH INDEPENDENT FRONT WHEEL SPRINGING AND STEERING

THE FIRST BRITISH CAR WITH AN ALL-SYNCHRO-MESH 4-SPEED GEARBOX

To-day ALVIS cars continue to lead in modern automobile design.

**ALVIS CAR & ENGINEERING CO. LTD.
COVENTRY**

THERE IS NO SUBSTITUTE FOR AN ALVIS

ALVIS

H.P.

ALVIVACITY PLUS

VISIBILITY

Every **ALVIS** car is designed to give speed with **SAFETY** as well as speed in **SILENCE**. Wide range visibility is an important necessity in a fast car . . . with no blind spots and the wings in full view. The above illustration is an actual photograph taken from the normal driving position in the **ALVIS** "Speed Twenty" and clearly shows the excellent visibility afforded. This attribute combined with the incorporation of independent front wheel springing and steering and the all-silent all-synchromesh four speed gearbox, definitely establishes new ideals in ease of control. "Speed 20" Models at prices from £700. Other Models from £490.

ALVIS CAR & ENGINEERING CO. LTD., COVENTRY

London Service Station: Great West Road, Brentford.

Distributors for London and Home Counties: Charles Follett Ltd., 18, Berkeley Street W.1.

"SPEED TWENTY"

ALVIS

SPEED WITH SAFETY

H.P.

See the 1936
ALVIS CARS
AT OLYMPIA
(STAND N° 83, MAIN HALL)

and keep in tune with modern life.

OLYMPIA presents the opportunity to inspect, *and try*, this most modern of motor cars for which there is no satisfactory substitute. There is no other car which combines its own distinctive qualities with the spirit of the age so successfully as the ALVIS.

Not only in style, speed and silence of operation does the ALVIS excel, but also in road-holding and cornering qualities due to the perfected system of independent front wheel springing and steering.

The new 3½ LITRE ALVIS is *the sensation of the Show,* described as the opening of a new chapter in automobile history. Do not miss this wonderful exhibit if you would keep up-to-date with engineering progress.

Illustrated particulars of 1936 Models from £490, post free from :

ALVIS CAR & ENGINEERING CO. LTD., COVENTRY.

London Service Station : Great West Road, Brentford.

Distributors for London and Home Counties : Charles Follett, Ltd., 18, Berkeley Street, W.1.

Shown at the Show

ON THE MAYFAIR STAND Nº 34
A BEAUTIFUL BODY
ON THE **NEW ALVIS**

Three-and-a-half Litre

HALLAM
OF
BIRMINGHAM
FOR
ALVIS

With long flowing lines—constructed from finest ash—body panelling in hand beaten aluminium —mounted on the strongest frame construction ever built—strength beyond all emergencies— scientific weight distribution, unhampered vision, silent smoothness and comfort wherever you sit—doors that will not rattle, modern windows with draught excluders fitted—built by craftsmen, richly and durably interpreted in distinctive design, minimising wind resistance yet giving deeply cushioned luxurious interior—a sunshine roof, trickle-proof—and an ingenious built-in luggage container adjustable for week-end or month.

ELEVEN SEVENTY-FIVE POUNDS

FRANK HALLAM, BRISTOL ST., BIRMINGHAM

Service facilities at Great West Road, Brentford, Middlesex.

CRAFTSMANSHIP THAT'S DISTINCTIVE

SPEED TWENTY

Tourer - - - **£795**

Sunshine Saloon **£895**

4-seated Coupé **£895**

One cannot fail to be impressed by the gracefully moulded curves and flowing lines achieved by this beautiful coachwork exclusively designed and built for Charles Follett by Vanden Plas. Nor is that all! Cunningly devised seating, headroom and legroom positions make it possible for *anyone* — no matter what his build—to recline in comfort, a point much appreciated on long journeys. Hidden away in the tail of each model is an exceptionally large luggage trunk. These are points that even a casual examination will reveal—but there are many others only a trial run will bring to light. We are anxious to place a car at your disposal—any distance— no obligation.

CHARLES FOLLETT LTD

SOLE DISTRIBUTORS FOR ALVIS IN LONDON AND HOME COUNTIES

18. BERKELEY ST. LONDON. W.I. *MAYFAIR 6266*

LONDON SERVICE STATION:- GREAT WEST ROAD, BRENTFORD. MIDDLESEX.

The finest 4 cyl. car ALVIS have ever built...

ALVIS

A four-cylinder car first made the name ALVIS famous. The unprecedented success of ALVIS 12/50 four-cylinder models in racing and in the hands of enthusiasts all over the world, has constituted one of the outstanding phases of post-war motoring history. The ALVIS "FIREBIRD"—successor to this line of famous models—is the finest four-cylinder car ALVIS have ever built.

Every detail of the "FIREBIRD" chassis reveals the brilliance of ALVIS engineering. Meticulous attention to the all-important question of weight distribution still further enhances the ALVIS reputation for perfect road-holding and safety under all conditions. These, and many other qualities, are exclusive to the ALVIS "FIREBIRD"—that is why every owner is such a great enthusiast. Price from £490.

ALVIS LONDON SHOWROOMS
are now open in Byron House, Nos. 7, 8 & 9, St. James's St.

Catalogues from
ALVIS Car & Engineering Co., Ltd., Coventry.
London Service Station: Great West Road, Brentford.

"FIREBIRD"

CRAFTSMANSHIP

IN EVERY DETAIL

Swift, Silent, Safe, and Superb in style this four-seater drop-head coupé Speed Twenty Alvis is an excellent dual-purpose car. It fulfils the requirements of a closed two-four-seater, and on the other hand offers a thrill which can only come from driving an open car of exceptionally high performance. The price is eight hundred and fifty pounds.

PRICES :—

Speed Twenty sports tourer	£700
Four-door saloon	£850
Crested Eagle (20 h.p.) four- or six-light saloon	£800
Limousine	£900
Silver Eagle (17 h.p.) four- or six-light saloon	£598
Firebird 14 h.p. four-light saloon ...	£510
Three-and-a-half Litre Chassis	£775

Supplementing Alvis sales with service worthy of the car, Frank Hallam offers demonstrations throughout the country without obligation to the enquirer. As Alvis Distributor he will deal favourably with any make of car in part exchange, and will give prompt delivery of new models.

The outlasting value given by Alvis cars is proved by the high-class selection of reliable used cars in stock.

TELEPHONE :
MIDLAND 2456-2457.

MIDLANDS DISTRIBUTOR

FRANK HALLAM

18-20 Bristol Street

BIRMINGHAM

JULY 1936

COGENT

A CAR IS NO BETTER THAN THE QUALITY OF ITS MANUFACTURE

ALVIS *Perfection*
IS NO CHANCE CREATION

Each piston and connecting rod is weighed and balanced, and each set carefully selected to ensure the smooth, silent running of every ALVIS.

Many years of building only to an ideal have produced a range of thoroughbred cars which are now supreme. In every detail the ALVIS is made to the highest standards of perfection. Of the many qualities exclusive to the new ALVIS cars, smoothness and silence allied with great speed and power are perhaps most noticeable. Here is another unbiased opinion :—

" The MORNING POST," Oliver Stewart, Feb. 17.

" **I do not know of any car in which high speed can be enjoyed with greater confidence and safety. I obtained a speedometer reading of 95 miles an hour, and the car at this speed is** *comfortable,* *silent and smooth.* **Seventy miles an hour can be reached in third, and when the engine is turning over fast it runs so smoothly that all evidence of its existence vanishes, except for the pull. In traffic the car behaves extremely well. I found that one could drop the speed to 7 m.p.h. in top gear, and then accelerate away right up the scale without snatch or fuss."**

1937 Models from £545

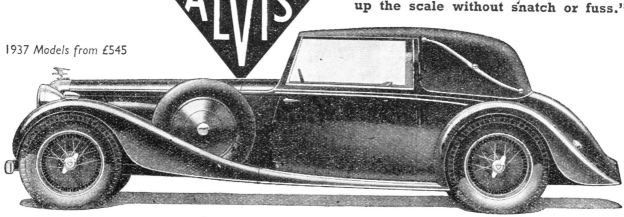

ALVIS, LTD., COVENTRY, and BYRON HOUSE, ST. JAMES'S STREET, LONDON, S.W.1.

THE INCOMPARABLE ALVIS, SUPPORTED BY A PERSONAL SERVICE

"CRESTED EAGLE" Saloon 20 h.p.
£800

The Alvis Crested Eagle has been designed to meet the demand of the thoughtful motorist who desires comfort with dignity, and yet wants a car capable of high speeds. Luxuriously equipped— upholstered with the finest hand-buffed hide—roomily designed, every thought has been given to the comfort of the occupants. Three coachwork styles are available, comprising the Four-light Saloon £800, Six-light Saloon £800 and the Limousine £900. Illustrated is the Six-light Saloon with comfortable seating accommodation for five people

For over ten years I have been the Alvis Midlands Distributor and my experience in general enables me to offer you any information or advice you may require concerning any make of car whether new or second-hand. Demonstrations can be arranged throughout the country with pleasure and without obligation.

MIDLAND DISTRIBUTOR   'PHONE: MIDLAND 2456-7

FRANK HALLAM
18-20 Bristol Street
BIRMINGHAM

Presenting
A NEW ALVIS
*true to type – yet
infinitely different*

The " SPEED TWENTY-FIVE " represents an entirely new conception of silent sports car performance *because* :—

It is superbly smooth and silent.
It has refinement in every detail.
It has really phenomenal acceleration.
It has the finest system of steering and suspension in the world.
It is utterly safe under any road conditions.
It has luxurious and distinctive coachwork.
It is the most comfortable sports car it is possible to buy.
The ALVIS " SPEED TWENTY-FIVE " costs from £700.

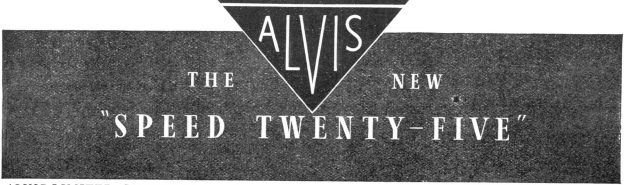

ALVIS

THE NEW

"SPEED TWENTY-FIVE"

ALVIS LIMITED, COVENTRY. *London Showrooms : Byron House, 7, 8, 9, St. James's St., S.W.1. 'Phone : WHI* 8506

SEPTEMBER 1936

THE NEW *Silver Crest*

ALVIS

The establishment of an ideal . . . .

A new and higher ideal has been established by the introduction of the new ALVIS six cylinder 20 H.P. SILVER CREST series (with the alternative of a 16.95 H.P. engine). These fine cars represent an outstanding combination of speed, safety and refinement, yet they are moderately priced. With their perfect suspension, easiest of all synchromesh gear changes, smooth, silent power units, amazing acceleration and high maximum speeds—that of the 20 H.P. being in excess of 80 m.p.h.—they will be found to meet every demand of modern road conditions.

The new SILVER CREST models with distinctive full five-seater coachwork are presented to a critical public only after ALVIS engineers have satisfied themselves that their efforts have attained the peak of perfection in the light of present-day knowledge. They take their place among the World's best motor cars. ALVIS—"MASTER OF THE KING'S HIGHWAY."

The AUTOCAR SAYS————————

"A remarkable combination of comfortable riding, excellent roadholding and accurate steering" . . . *WITH ALVIS PERFORMANCE*

20 h.p. Models from £595
(Alternative 16.95 h.p. Models from £565)

THE DESIRE FOR THE BEST

THE desire for the best dominates the whole **ALVIS** organisation. Their tradition has been, and is, to build as nearly the perfect motor car as is humanly possible. Neither time nor expense is spared.

ALVIS, true to this tradition, designed their present range of smooth, silent, high performance cars. Britain's finest coachmakers acknowledged that tradition when they combined sweeping, graceful, modern lines with the dignity which is **ALVIS.** The result is a series of cars unsurpassed in distinction, luxury, speed and security.   Prices from £545.

ALVIS LTD., HOLYHEAD ROAD, COVENTRY *and at* BYRON HOUSE, 7-9 ST. JAMES' STREET, LONDON, S.W.1

REPUTATION UNEQUALLED
SUPREMACY UNQUESTIONED

12-50

12-60

AND NOW *The new* **12-70**

ALVIS

From the year of its creation the 12/50 ALVIS stood supremely alone. Wherever British motoring prestige was attacked, ALVIS proved a worthy acceptor of the challenge.

And today, after constant experiment, ALVIS are proud to announce the new 12/70 4-Cylinder Model—a car designed to uphold and enhance that brilliant reputation—that unquestioned supremacy.

Characteristic ALVIS high speed performance, beauty of line and safety are but a few of its outstanding merits. Prices from £435. Write for full details.

Master · of · the · King's · Highway

ALVIS LTD., COVENTRY. *Phone:* 5501; and at BYRON HOUSE, ST. JAMES'S STREET, LONDON, S.W.1. *Whitehall* 8506

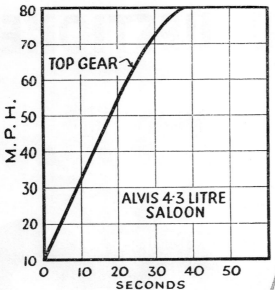
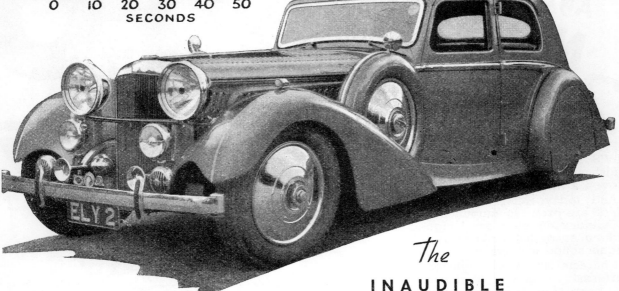

BEAUTY WITH BRILLIANT PERFORMANCE

Sidney Henschel, writing in the "Financial News" on March 4th, 1938, says :

". . Now, as always, the ALVIS is an individual car of beauty and brilliant performance — British automobile craftsmanship at its best."

There are ALVIS dealers in all centres who are anxious to demonstrate to you the outstanding qualities of this brilliant car.

	16.95 h.p.	20 h.p.
4-light Saloon	£565	£595
6-light Saloon	£565	£595
Drophead Coupe	£575	£605

Engineers and motorists of long experience know and appreciate the many qualities in design and performance that, whatever the price they pay, they can only find in an ALVIS. For perfect smoothness with complete silence, extreme simplicity of control, rock steady steering and road-holding at all speeds . . .

THERE IS NO OTHER CAR QUITE LIKE AN ALVIS

ALVIS LTD., COVENTRY (Tel. 5501); and at BYRON HOUSE, 7-9 ST. JAMES'S STREET, LONDON, S.W.1. (Tel. Whitehall 8506)

APRIL 1938

77

R.A.C. RALLY

BRIGHTON
COACHWORK COMPETITION

— PREMIER AWARD —

The Premier Award for the best open car irrespective of price, The Sussex Cup, was won by Miss Dorothy Stanley-Turner's

100 m.p.h. 4·3 LITRE ALVIS

SPECIAL SHORT CHASSIS OPEN SPORTS TOURER

Also winner of Class 5a

(subject to official confirmation)

ALVIS

Alvis Limited, Coventry.   (Phone: Coventry 5501).   London Showrooms: 7/9 St. James's St., S.W.1 (WHI 8506)

THE IMPROVED

12-70

Saloon £435

Many detailed improvements have been made to the 12/70 h.p. Alvis, and the equipment of this model is now on the same luxurious scale as the larger cars in the range. The radiator now has a vertical grille and the headlamps have been increased in size and efficiency. The seating has been redesigned and is now fitted with Dunlopillo Overlay Upholstery. Other new equipment includes rear bumpers and twin wind horns. Its maximum of over 80 m.p.h., with its superlative roadholding, enables the 12/70 to put up very high average speeds in the utmost comfort and safety. Saloon £435. Drophead Coupe £445. Sports 4-seater £425.

ALVIS LTD., COVENTRY.   LONDON SHOWROOMS· 7-9 ST. JAMES'S STREET, S.W.1. · TEL.: WHITEHALL 8506

Individuality

THE FOURTEEN Four-light Saloon ex works £855

ALVIS LTD., COVENTRY   *Purchase Tax £238 . 5 . 0*

INDIVIDUALITY

" Typical of all that is

best in British high-class design, the new Alvis

Fourteen is a well-balanced four-door

saloon of generous capacity"

AUTOCAR NOV. 15, 46

FOUR DOOR FOUR LIGHT SALOON ex works £855
PURCHASE TAX £238 · 5s. ALVIS LTD. COVENTRY

ALVIS TICKFORD D.H. COUPÉ

COACHWORK DE LUXE
by **TICKFORD**

LONDON SHOWROOMS:
TICKFORD LTD. 6-9 UPPER SAINT MARTIN'S LANE
LONDON W. C. 2
WORKS: NEWPORT PAGNELL · BUCKS.

COACHWORK DE LUXE BY
TICKFORD
ON ALVIS FOURTEEN

LONDON SHOWROOMS: TICKFORD LTD. 6-9 UPPER SAINT MARTIN'S LANE, LONDON. W. C. 2.
WORKS: NEWPORT PAGNELL · BUCKS.

The
ALVIS
FOURTEEN
The Enthusiast's Motor Car

HWK 667

Fast cornering is a feature of the ALVIS Fourteen performance. The car holds the road beautifully at speed, without roll or sway, and the feeling of confidence engendered by ample power, the ability to steer over a sixpence and the knowledge that the brakes are powerful and suspension well balanced is an aid to better and more enjoyable driving

STAND 170 *at the Motor Show, Earls Court*

ALVIS LIMITED · COVENTRY · ENGLAND

FOURTEEN

D 30

ALVIS *Individuality*

"The 'Fourteen' adds to the
typical ALVIS performance
on the road, a degree of
all-round refinement which
is quite impeccable."

Autocar, November 15th, 1946

ALVIS LIMITED. COVENTRY

Individuality

A striking combination of graceful lines and quiet, effortless performance the Alvis Fourteen Special Sports Tourer has, embodied in its design, all the famous qualities of the true Alvis tradition with its reputation for the highest quality workmanship, high performance and utmost reliability under exacting conditions, with a strikingly beautiful but practical body

ALVIS   LIMITED   ·   COVENTRY   ·   ENGLAND

Individuality

THE NEW ALVIS
Three Litre is a notable
contribution to gracious
motoring. It combines a
design and performance
ahead of its time, with
the individual appearance
which has always
characterised an ALVIS
car.

The New Alvis Three Litre

ALVIS LIMITED · COVENTRY · ENGLAND

A.L.2

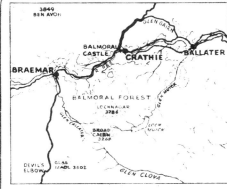

For the sheer joy of driving...
I'd like to go there in an

ALVIS

Across Balmoral Forest

the snow-bright range of Lochnagar rises high above Deeside. Along these roads to Braemar the Clans gather in September. And there, of course, the loyal and devoted clan of ALVIS drivers will be worthily represented. In the words of "*The Autocar*" Road Test February 15th, 1952 . . .

"An experienced and critical driver will not fail to be impressed by the feel of the car ; its handling qualities at both high and low speeds are much above the average."

Photograph by courtesy of the British Travel & Holidays Association

89

ALVIS LTD · COVENTRY
THREE LITRE: SALOON · DROP HEAD COUPÉ

AL 25

P E R F E C T I O N

ALVIS

THE Alvis T.C. 21/100 Drophead Coupé is a masterly example of British car-making at its individual best — built by the practice and skill of craftsmen working as a team; built for the man who asks not only for stylish individuality but for the power of performance and the challenge of speed under perfect control. Here then is yet another great-hearted car to be proudly owned and driven mile after mile, year after year. As the "Motor" says of the T.C. 21/100, "This is the way to go motoring! The new Alvis T.C. 21/100 offers delightful motoring with a maximum speed of 100 miles per hour, 85 miles per hour in third, and a petrol consumption of 22 miles per gallon at a constant 60 miles per hour. In traffic, it will amble quietly in top, or will leap away in its indirect gears in a manner which at first almost disconcerts by the ease with which it does it. Like all really good enthusiasts' cars, the T.C. 21/100 flatters the man who handles it."

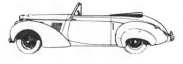 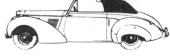 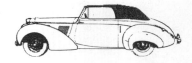

The three-position Melloroid hood and Smiths air conditioning unit makes for motoring comfort from January to December. Let it shine, and the hood can be neatly folded away as an open tourer. Let it pour, and you drive in all the warmth and deep-sprung comfort of a saloon.

A L V I S

ALVIS LIMITED, HOLYHEAD ROAD, COVENTRY

ALSOA

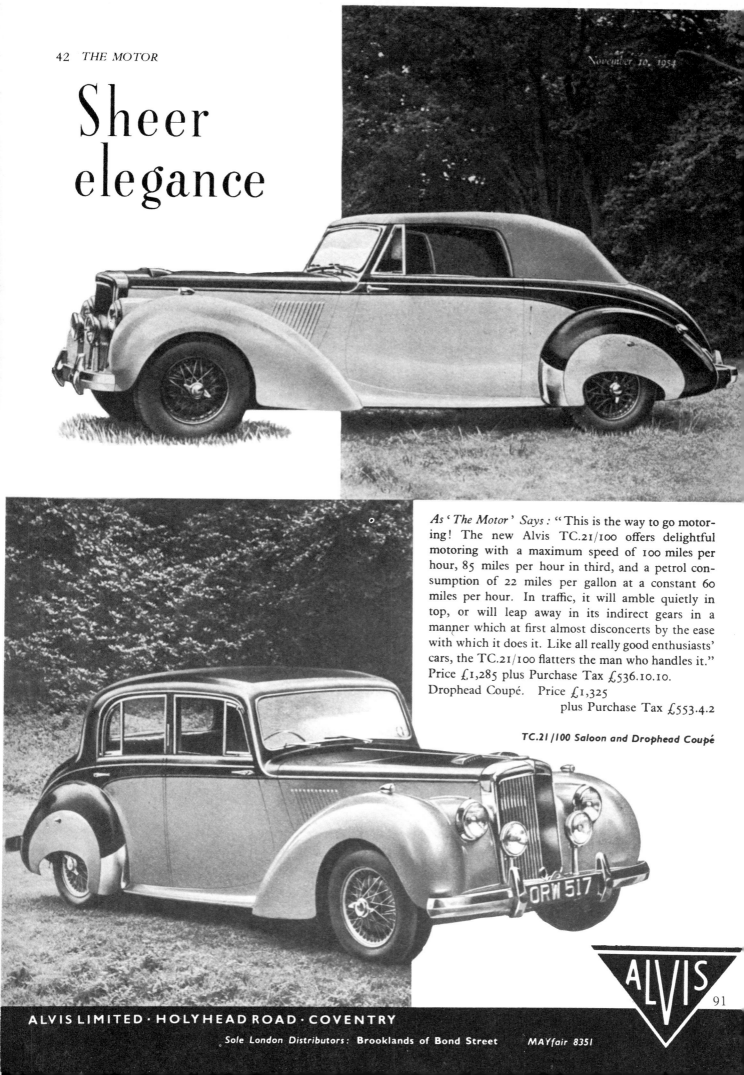

We've both come a long way...

ALVIS **1920**

1955

Styled by Carrosserie Graber of Berne,
this 100 m.p.h. saloon is the finest Alvis yet.

ALVIS OF COVENTRY

Sole London Distributors: BROOKLANDS OF BOND STREET   *Telephone:* MAYfair 8351

AL64

Tailor-made motoring

Coachwork by Park Ward—styled by Graber—engineered by Alvis. This particularly happy combination has resulted in a car that will have a strong appeal to those who appreciate high quality, good planning and a better than 100 miles per hour performance. Two models are available: a four to five seater saloon and a stylish four seater drophead coupé.

COUPÉ £3,293 . 17 . 0 *Inc.*

ALVIS

THREE LITRE SALOON & COUPÉ

Coachwork by Park Ward

ALVIS

THREE LITRE SALOON & DROP-HEAD COUPÉ

COACHWORK BY PARK WARD

Three Litre Saloon, *Basic Price* £1,995.0.0. *Purchase Tax* £832.7.6.　£2,827.7.6.

Three Litre Drop-Head Coupé *Basic Price* £2,195.0.0. *Purchase Tax* £915.14.2. £3,110.14.2.

Both cars fitted with Lockheed Disc Brakes as standard; Borg Warner Automatic Transmission available at £134.11.8 extra, including tax.

95

STAND NO. 121 EARLS COURT

ALVIS THREE LITRE SERIES III

Improved performance and re-styling are features of the new Alvis Series III Saloon and Drophead Coupe which are being shown for the first time at Earls Court this year. The Graber-styled body has been given a new frontal design, incorporating a twin headlamp system. Steering and front suspension have been modified to give better handling, and engine power has been increased to 130 B.H.P. at 5,000 R.P.M., giving improved top speed and acceleration characteristics.

* 5-speed all-synchromesh gearbox fitted as standard.

SERIES III SALOON
£2,773 · 13 · 9 inc. P.T.

SERIES III
DROPHEAD COUPE
£3,015 · 7 · 1 inc. P.T.

ALVIS OF COVENTRY · SOLE LONDON DISTRIBUTORS: BROOKLANDS OF BOND STREET · TELEPHONE: MAYFAIR 8351